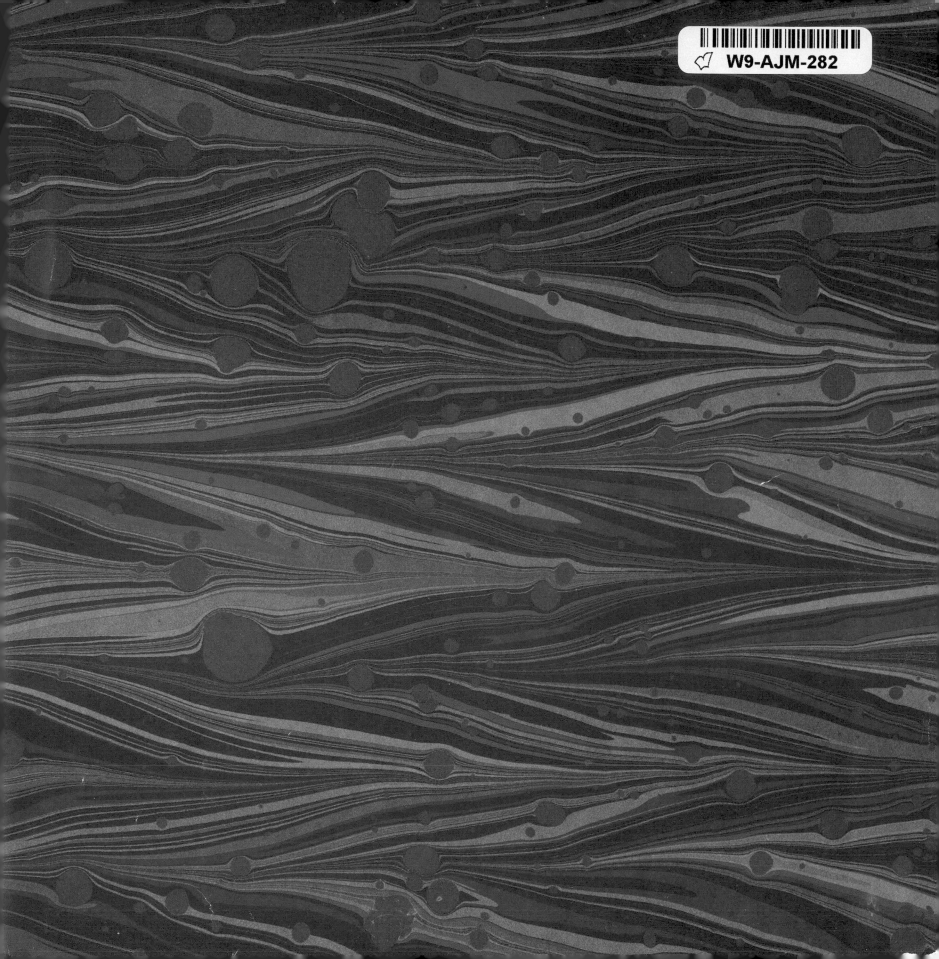

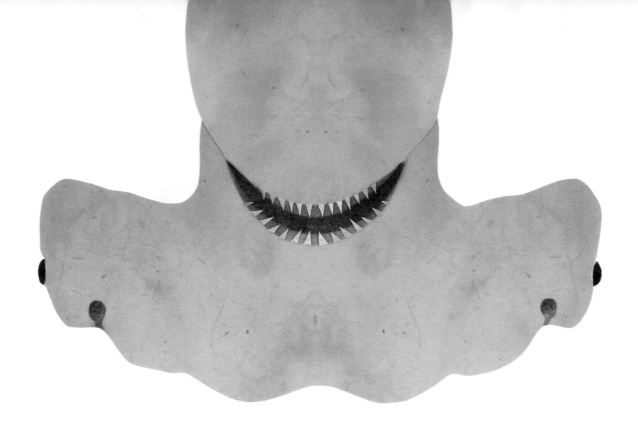

For Alec and Jamie

The illustrations are torn- and cut-paper collage.
The text is typeset in Felt Tip Woman and Proxima Nova.

ISBN 978-1-328-56949-3

Manufactured in USA
PHX 4500824290

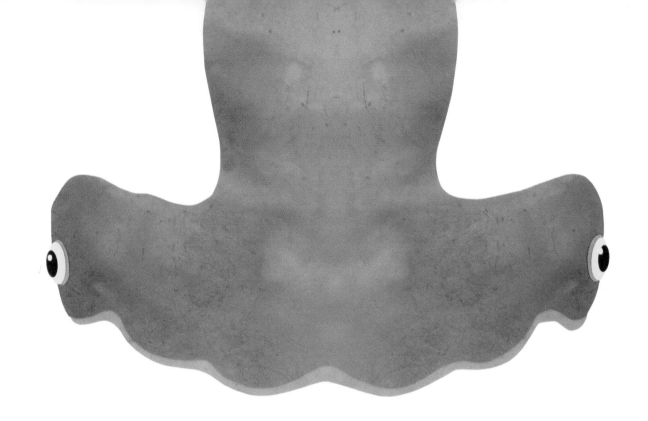

The Shark Book

Steve Jenkins &
Robin Page

Houghton Mifflin Harcourt • Boston • New York

Whether they deserve it or not, sharks are among the most feared animals on earth. These fish are almost perfect predators, and they've been pursuing their prey in the oceans for over 400 million years. Some are big, fast, and dangerous, with powerful jaws filled with razor-sharp teeth. Others are gentle giants, cruising slowly through the sea as they feed on shrimp and other tiny animals. The largest shark is as big as a bus, while the smallest could fit in the palm of your hand. Some of the strangest and most unfamiliar sharks live in deep, dark waters and are almost never seen by humans.

A shiver of sharks

Some sharks spend their lives on the seafloor. Others cruise the open ocean, or hunt in shallow coastal waters. A few even live in freshwater lakes and rivers. There are more than 500 different kinds of sharks.

epaulette shark

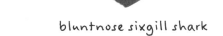

bluntnose sixgill shark

whale shark

frilled shark

common thresher shark

goblin shark

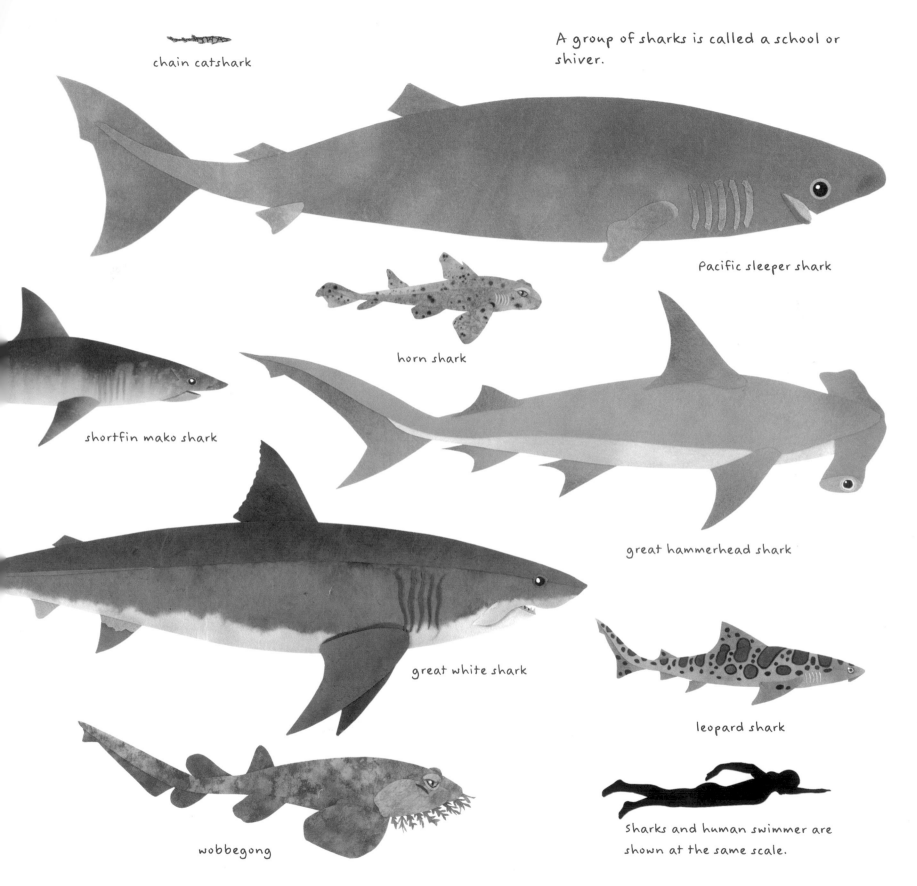

chain catshark

A group of sharks is called a school or shiver.

Pacific sleeper shark

horn shark

shortfin mako shark

great hammerhead shark

great white shark

leopard shark

wobbegong

Sharks and human swimmer are shown at the same scale.

What is a shark?

Sharks are fish. But unlike most other kinds of fish, sharks don't have bones. Their skeletons are made of cartilage, the same material found in your nose and ear lobes. Cartilage weighs less than bone, and a lighter and more flexible skeleton allows a shark to move more quickly.

Shark bodies vary in size and shape, but many are sleek and streamlined to reduce water resistance.

This is a **blue shark**.

The shark's large tail propels it through the water. A typical shark's tail is larger on the top than on the bottom.

In scary movies about sharks, the dorsal fin is often shown knifing through the water. This fin's purpose is to keep the shark's body upright and prevent it from rolling from side to side.

Most sharks have darker backs and lighter bellies. This is called countershading, and it helps the shark blend in with the dark water below and bright surface above.

Sharks have a lateral line—a row of pressure-sensitive openings—that runs along their body. The lateral line can detect vibrations in the water created by prey or other predators.

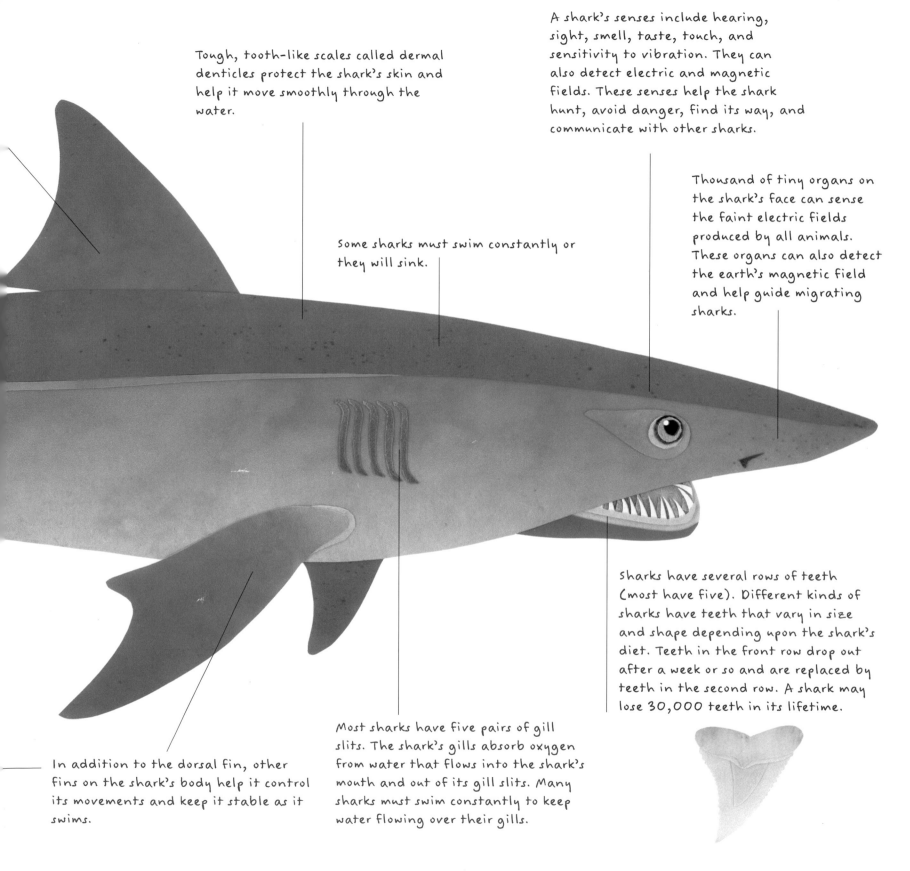

Tough, tooth-like scales called dermal denticles protect the shark's skin and help it move smoothly through the water.

A shark's senses include hearing, sight, smell, taste, touch, and sensitivity to vibration. They can also detect electric and magnetic fields. These senses help the shark hunt, avoid danger, find its way, and communicate with other sharks.

Thousand of tiny organs on the shark's face can sense the faint electric fields produced by all animals. These organs can also detect the earth's magnetic field and help guide migrating sharks.

Some sharks must swim constantly or they will sink.

Sharks have several rows of teeth (most have five). Different kinds of sharks have teeth that vary in size and shape depending upon the shark's diet. Teeth in the front row drop out after a week or so and are replaced by teeth in the second row. A shark may lose 30,000 teeth in its lifetime.

In addition to the dorsal fin, other fins on the shark's body help it control its movements and keep it stable as it swims.

Most sharks have five pairs of gill slits. The shark's gills absorb oxygen from water that flows into the shark's mouth and out of its gill slits. Many sharks must swim constantly to keep water flowing over their gills.

Big and little

The whale shark—the largest living shark—is also the biggest fish in the sea. The smallest shark could fit on a dinner plate. Megalodon was the largest shark of them all. It lived millions of years ago, and it could have killed and eaten anything in the sea, including a whale.

dwarf lantern shark

Stethacanthus

wobbegong

megalodon

basking shark

great hammerhead shark

Sarcoprion

These sharks—and the human swimmer—are shown at the same scale. Extinct sharks are gray; living sharks are blue.

blue shark

horn shark

shortfin mako shark

common thresher shark

adult human

great white shark

tiger shark

blacktip reef shark

whale shark

Orthacanthus

9

Born alive . . .

Most sharks give birth to live young. Newborn sharks are called pups.

Shark mothers and fathers do not care for their offspring. In fact, baby sharks must often avoid being eaten by their parents.

This is a **sand tiger shark** inside its mother's womb. The pup started out with ten or twelve brothers and sisters, but the largest of these unborn sharks survived by eating all of its smaller siblings.

Spiny dogfish sharks are born alive in litters that average six or seven pups. These sharks spend up to 24 months in the womb. They are born with a yolk sac—their source of food in the womb—still attached.

. . . or hatched from an egg

Some sharks lay eggs that will hatch later. Shark eggs are enclosed in egg cases that are sometimes called mermaid's purses or devil's purses. Each case contains one egg. The egg cases on this page are shown at actual size.

The tendrils on a **swell shark** egg case wrap themselves around rocks or plants to prevent the egg case from drifting away.

To keep her egg safe, a mother **Port Jackson shark** takes her egg case in her mouth and wedges the case into a crack in the rocks.

A baby **greater spotted catshark** and the yolk that it feeds on can be seen inside this translucent egg case.

What do sharks eat?

All sharks are carnivores—they eat other animals—and they consume a wide variety of prey. The unusual diet of one shark, the bonnethead, includes seagrass as well as animals.

The whale shark, megamouth shark, and **basking shark** (shown at left) are filter feeders. They often swim slowly with an open mouth, straining zooplankton and small fish from the water. Despite their size, these sharks are harmless to humans.

The basking shark is the second-largest shark—and the second-largest fish—in the world.

zooplankton—shrimp and other tiny animals

Tiger sharks, great white sharks, and other open-ocean hunters prefer to eat seals, sea lions, and other animals that are high in fat. They also feed on the carcasses of dead whales.

When most people think of a shark, they are imagining a large, fierce, fast-swimming fish such as a great white, blue, bull, or **tiger shark** (shown here).

The tiger shark attacks at high speed, ramming its prey—fish, turtles, dolphins, and marine mammals such as seals—with its jaws open. The shark bites down, then shakes its body from side to side to tear off a large piece of flesh.

FLORIDA
SHRK826

Tiger sharks swallow almost anything they can fit into their mouth. Bottles, shoes, toys, and license plates have all been found in a tiger shark's stomach.

Whip, gulp, and chomp

Some sharks employ unusual hunting and feeding techniques.

The tail of the **bigeye thresher shark** can be as long as its body. This shark hunts schools of bluefish or mackerel, using its tail as a whip to stun or kill the smaller fish.

The **smoothback angel shark** is an ambush hunter. It lies quietly on the seafloor, partially covered with sand or mud. When a fish, squid, crab, or other prey animal comes close, the angel shark lunges and seizes its victim with needle-sharp teeth.

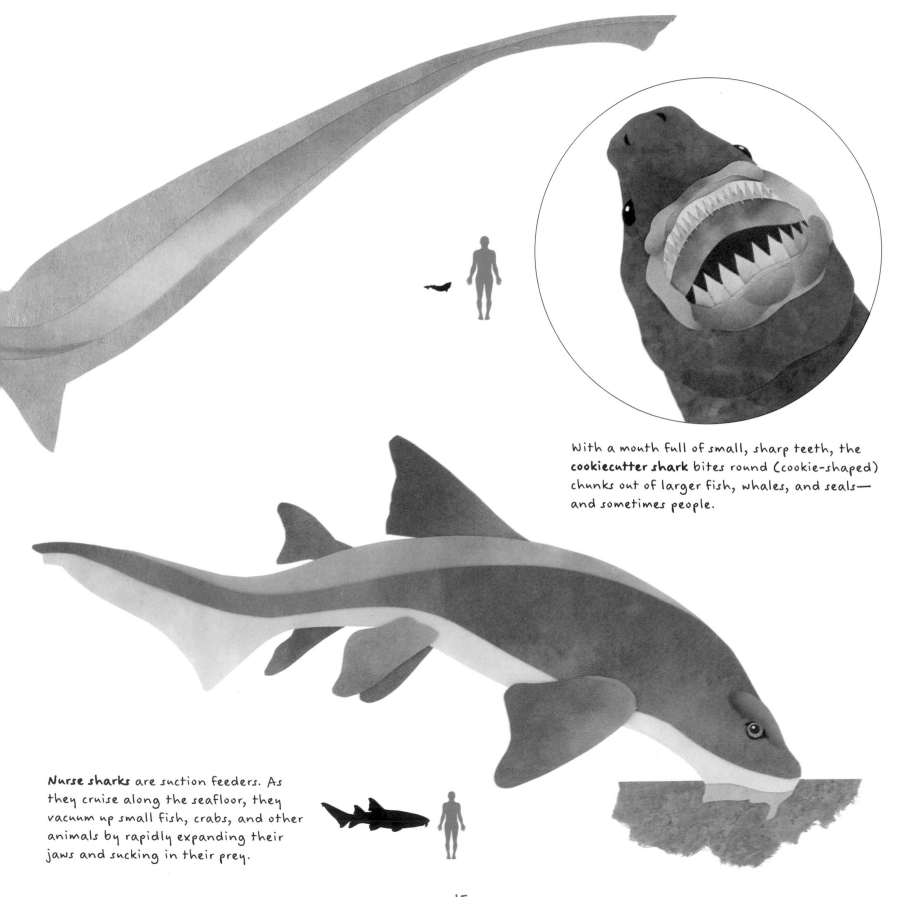

With a mouth full of small, sharp teeth, the **cookiecutter shark** bites round (cookie-shaped) chunks out of larger fish, whales, and seals— and sometimes people.

Nurse sharks are suction feeders. As they cruise along the seafloor, they vacuum up small fish, crabs, and other animals by rapidly expanding their jaws and sucking in their prey.

Jaws!

The **great white shark**, the largest predatory fish in the sea, is also the most well known of all sharks. It may not deserve its reputation as a ruthless man-eater, but it is still a formidable predator.

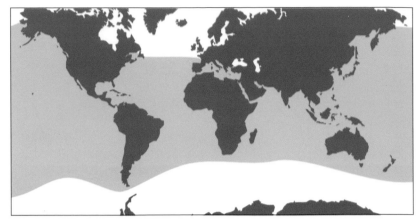

Great white sharks can move quickly when they need to, reaching speeds of 25 miles per hour (40 kilometers per hour) in short bursts.

Great whites can be found throughout much of the world's oceans, but they spend most of their time in coastal waters. These sharks sometimes swim thousands of miles to find a mate or new feeding grounds.

The great white hunts seals by lurking deep in the water. When it spots a seal, it swims upward, grabbing the seal and bursting out of the water. This is called "breaching."

Though attacks on humans are rare, great whites have been responsible for some 350 attacks—more than any other species of shark.

The great white shark can detach its upper jaw from its skull, allowing it to open its mouth extra wide. Its teeth have sharp, jagged edges, ideal for slicing through flesh and bone.

The great white (and a few other sharks) has the unusual ability to raise its body temperature, making parts of its body as much as 25°F (14°C) warmer than the surrounding water. Warm muscles are more efficient and help these sharks swim faster.

Big Fish

The whale shark is the world's largest fish. It is a filter feeder, straining shrimp, small fish, and other animals from the water as it swims.

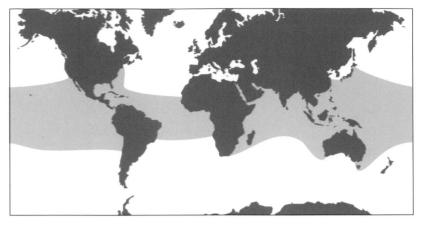

Whale sharks inhabit warm ocean waters around the world. They are migratory, sometimes traveling thousand of miles to their feeding grounds.

A whale shark's mouth can be five feet (1 1/2 meters) wide.

Despite their size, whale sharks are gentle and don't threaten humans.

Whale sharks may live to be over 100 years old.

A head like a hammer

The **great hammerhead shark** is the largest species of hammerhead. These sharks prey on fish, squid, crabs, rays, and other animals that live on or near the seafloor. Scientists speculate that the unusual shape of the shark's head and the location of its eyes aid the shark's vision as it hunts.

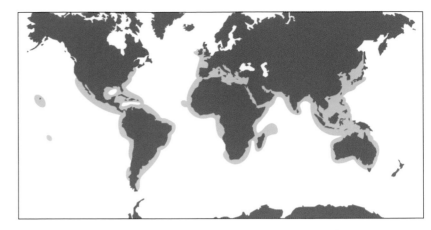

The great hammerhead shark is found in coastal waters throughout much of the world.

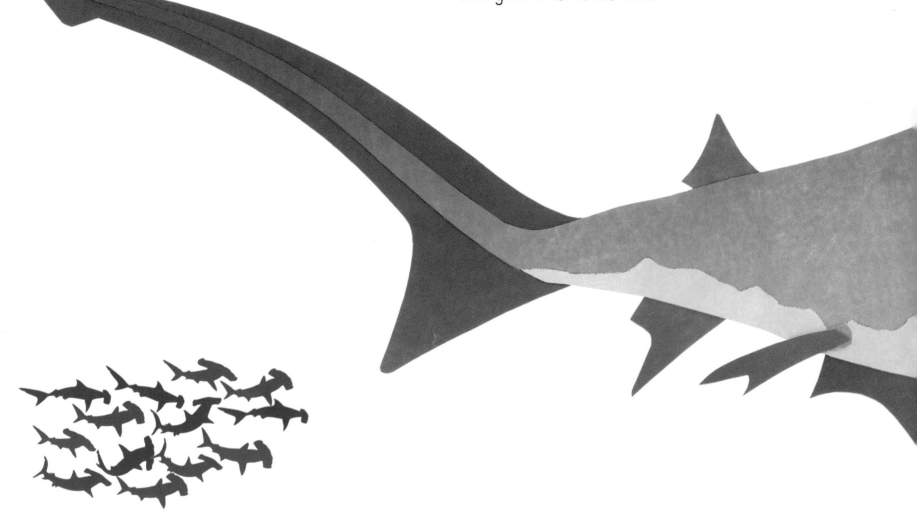

Scalloped hammerheads sometimes form schools of hundreds of sharks.

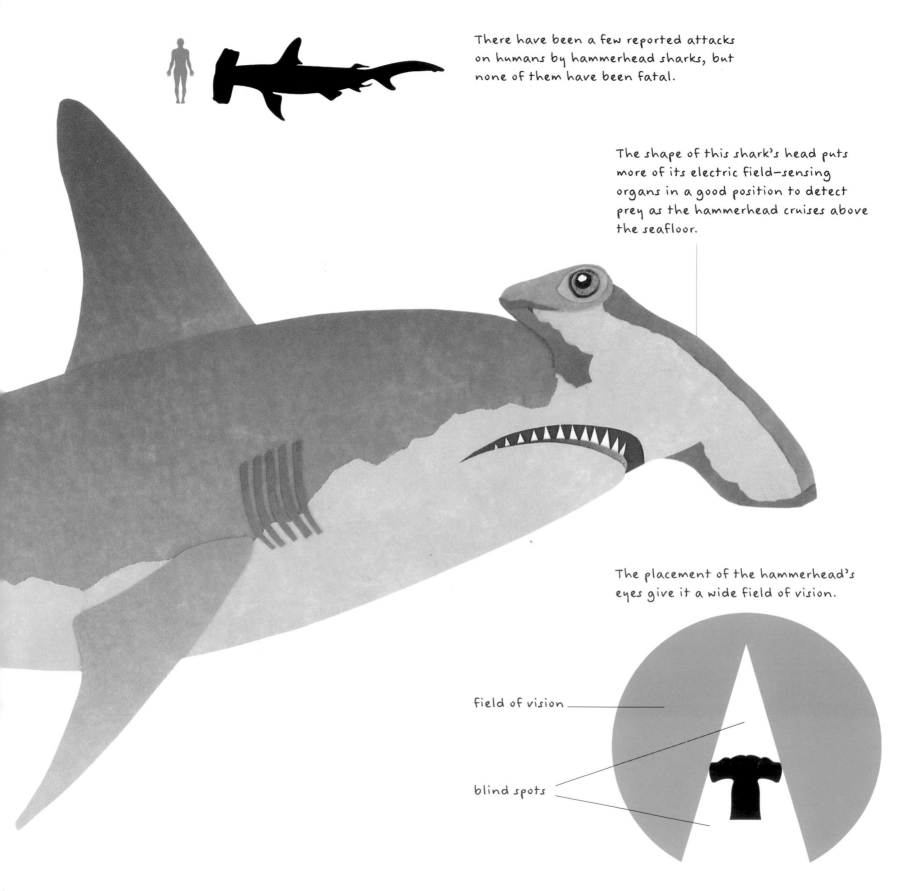

There have been a few reported attacks on humans by hammerhead sharks, but none of them have been fatal.

The shape of this shark's head puts more of its electric field-sensing organs in a good position to detect prey as the hammerhead cruises above the seafloor.

The placement of the hammerhead's eyes give it a wide field of vision.

field of vision

blind spots

Three peculiar fish

These sharks are rarely seen by humans. They live in deep ocean waters, and they are not a threat to people. They each have some unusual features that help them as they hunt.

The **goblin shark** lives in deep, dark water. Its long snout is covered in pits that can sense the faint electric fields that all animals produce. When it locates a fish or other prey, the goblin shark thrusts its jaws forward and grabs its victim.

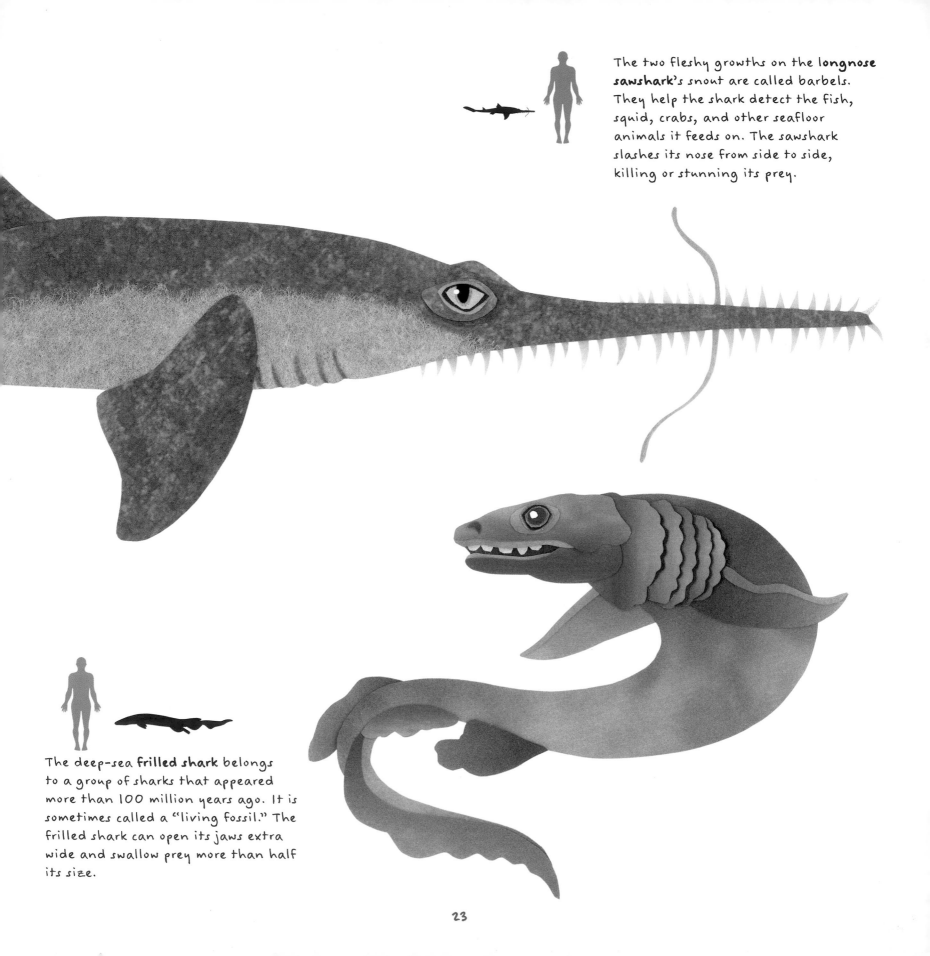

The two fleshy growths on the **longnose sawshark**'s snout are called barbels. They help the shark detect the fish, squid, crabs, and other seafloor animals it feeds on. The sawshark slashes its nose from side to side, killing or stunning its prey.

The deep-sea **frilled shark** belongs to a group of sharks that appeared more than 100 million years ago. It is sometimes called a "living fossil." The frilled shark can open its jaws extra wide and swallow prey more than half its size.

23

Glow-in-the-dark sharks

Many ocean-dwelling animals can light up. These two sharks make light in different ways and use it for different reasons.

The **velvet belly lantern shark** is bioluminescent—it produces its own light. When seen from below, its glowing belly matches the light coming from the surface, hiding the little shark from its predators.

The **chain catshark** gets its name from its green, catlike eyes. This shark is biofluorescent—it doesn't produce its own light, but absorbs and re-emits sunlight. Its greenish glow may serve to communicate with other catsharks.

Adaptable sharks

Most sharks spend their entire lives in the ocean. But there are a few that venture into unexpected places.

The **bull shark** has been responsible for more than 100 attacks on humans, many of them fatal. One of the most unusual things about this shark is its ability to survive in fresh water. It has been found in rivers more than 1,000 miles (1,600 kilometers) from the sea.

The **epaulette shark** spends much of its time in shallow tide pools, where it hunts worms, crabs, and other animals. It can "walk" from one tide pool to another, using its fins to drag itself across the rocks.

Ancient relatives

Since sharks first evolved more than 400 million years ago, many strange and awe-inspiring members of the shark family have come and gone. Because shark skeletons are made of cartilage instead of bone, they are seldom preserved as fossils. Much of what we know about ancient sharks is based on their fossilized teeth.

The most impressive shark of all was **megalodon**. It first prowled the oceans 16 million years ago, and went extinct about 1 1/2 million years ago. It might have looked like an oversize great white shark.

Helicoprion lived about 290 million years ago. Its most unusual feature was its buzz saw of a jaw, with as many as 150 teeth arranged in a spiral.

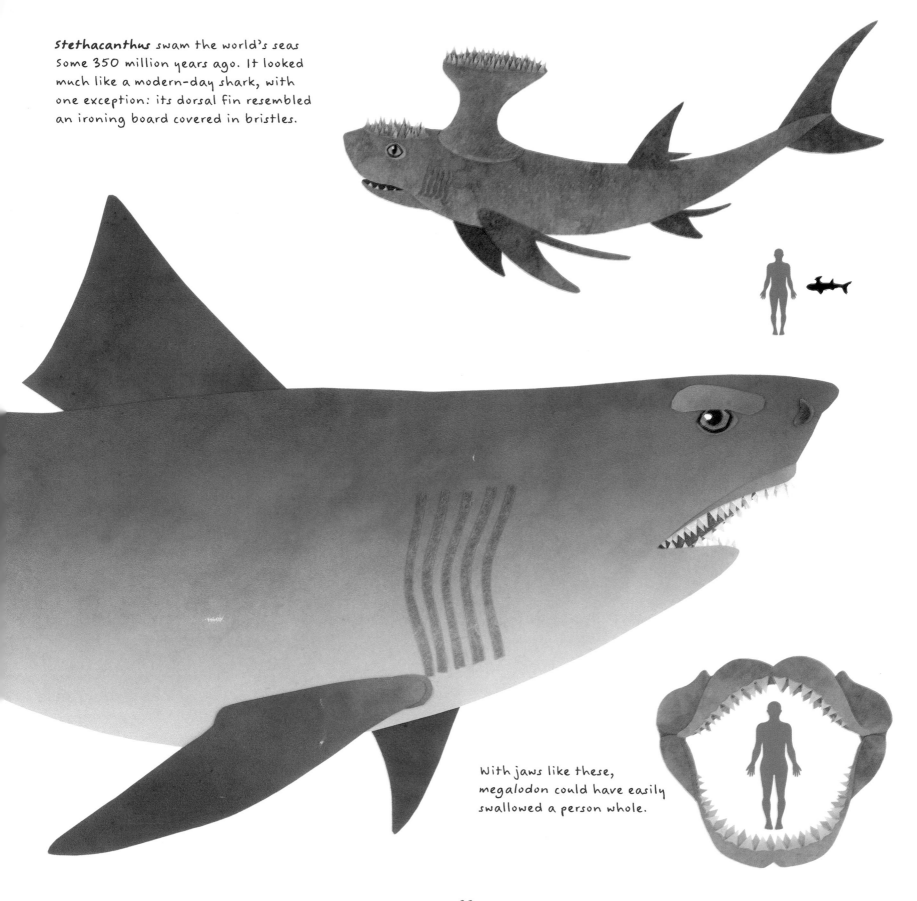

Stethacanthus swam the world's seas
some 350 million years ago. It looked
much like a modern-day shark, with
one exception: its dorsal fin resembled
an ironing board covered in bristles.

With jaws like these,
megalodon could have easily
swallowed a person whole.

Shark record holders

One **Greenland shark** has lived to more than 270 years of age. Some scientists believe that these sharks can live to be 500 years old.

The **shortfin mako** is the fastest shark, reaching speeds of 45 miles per hour (72 kilometers per hour) or more. It can also leap 30 feet (9 meters) above the ocean's surface—higher than any other shark.

The world's most common shark is the **spiny dogfish**. It gets its name from the venomous spines in front of each of its dorsal fins and its practice of hunting in packs (like dogs).

The world's largest shark, the **whale shark,** holds multiple records. It has the largest litter—one female whale shark was found with 300 pups in her womb. The whale shark also migrates the farthest. One individual was tracked for more than 12,000 miles (19,312 kilometers) across the Pacific Ocean.

The **great white shark** has the largest teeth of any living shark. Here a great white tooth is shown life-size with a much larger tooth from **megalodon**, an extinct relative that was the largest shark that has ever lived.

The largest school of sharks ever observed was a gathering of 1,400 **basking sharks** off the coast of New England.

The **Portuguese dogfish** has been found at depths of 12,057 feet (3,675 meters)—the greatest depth of any shark.

The tiny **pocket shark** is the rarest shark. Only two have ever been seen.

size comparison

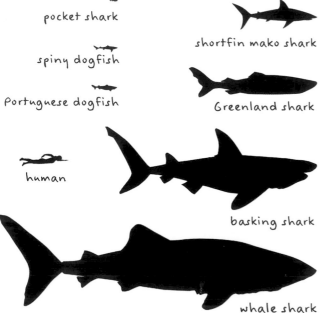

pocket shark

spiny dogfish

Portuguese dogfish

human

shortfin mako shark

Greenland shark

basking shark

whale shark

Shark attacks

About 80 unprovoked shark attacks are reported around the world every year. On average, seven of these attacks are fatal.

In the same period, several thousand people are killed by lightning and thousands more drown. Rip tides are much more dangerous than sharks.

It's likely that some shark attacks in undeveloped parts of the world go unreported, but they are still rare.

Of the more than 500 species of shark, just three are responsible for most of the attacks on humans.

The **great white shark** has attacked and killed more people than any other kind of shark.*
(350 attacks, 80 of them fatal)

The aggressive **tiger shark** is the second-most dangerous shark.
(111 attacks, 34 of them fatal)

The **bull shark** hunts in shallow ocean water and freshwater rivers where encounters with people are more likely. It's the third-most dangerous shark.
(100 attacks, 27 of them fatal)

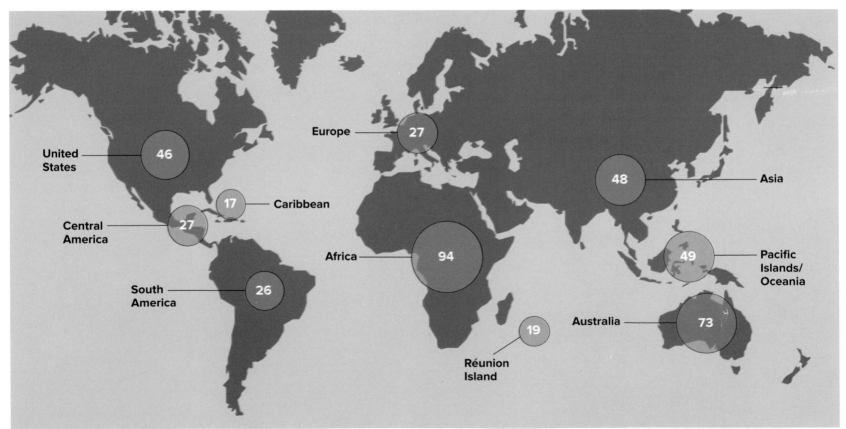

Sixty years of fatal shark attacks—the top ten locations

(Source: International Shark Attack File, 1958–2018)

*according to recorded unprovoked attacks since 1580

Sharks in danger

Sharks kill about seven people every year. But in the same period of time, humans kill an estimated 100 million sharks. They are killed for food, for sport, and as bycatch—the accidental victims of commercial fishing. Shark populations have decreased dramatically, and many species are at risk of extinction. Sharks are the top predators in their habitats. If they disappear, entire food webs can collapse and many other species will be lost.

Here are four of the most endangered sharks.

The **smoothback angel shark** was once common in the Atlantic Ocean and Mediterranean Sea. It is an unintended victim of commercial fishing, and it has almost vanished.

The **natal shyshark** is found in one small area off the coast of South Africa. It gets its name from its habit of curling up with its tail over its face if it feels threatened. Overfishing and pollution have left only a few of these sharks in the wild.

The **scalloped hammerhead** lives in warm ocean waters throughout the world. It is caught and killed in great numbers for its fins, which are considered a delicacy in Asia.

The **Ganges shark** lives in the rivers of northern India. Overfishing and pollution have pushed this rare freshwater shark to the edge of extinction.

This table shows the size, range, danger to humans, and conservation status* of the sharks in this book.

page number	name	average adult body length	range	dangerous to humans?	conservation status
cover, 5, 9, 16–17, 29, 30	**great white shark**	20 ft (6 m)	worldwide except for polar seas	yes	vulnerable
copyright page, 1, 20, 31	**scalloped hammerhead shark**	15 ft (5 m)	warm coastal waters worldwide	no	critically endangered
3, 25, 30	**bull shark**	8 ft (2½ m)	coastal areas of warm oceans, freshwater rivers, and lakes	yes	near threatened
4, 25	**epaulette shark**	22 in (56 cm)	Pacific Ocean around New Guinea and northern Australia	no	least concern
4	**bluntnose sixgill shark**	12 ft (3¾ m)	temperate coastal waters worldwide	no	near threatened
4, 8–9, 18–19, 28–29	**whale shark**	40 ft (12 m)	warm and tropical waters worldwide	no	endangered
4, 23	**frilled shark**	6½ ft (2 m)	scattered deep-water locations worldwide	no	least concern
4, 9	**common thresher shark**	20 ft (6 m)	warm and temperate waters worldwide	no	vulnerable
4, 22	**goblin shark**	13 ft (4 m)	probably worldwide, mostly in deep water	no	least concern
5, 24	**chain catshark**	2 ft (61 cm)	Northwest Atlantic, Gulf of Mexico, and Caribbean Sea	no	least concern
5	**Pacific sleeper shark**	12 ft (3½ m)	Arctic and temperate waters of the North Pacific	no	data deficient
5, 9	**horn shark**	3½ ft (1 m)	coastal waters of California to the Gulf of California	no	data deficient
4–5, 9, 28–29	**shortfin mako shark**	10 ft (3 m)	temperate and tropical waters worldwide	yes	endangered
5, 8–9, 20–21	**great hammerhead shark**	15 ft (4½ m)	tropical waters worldwide	unlikely	critically endangered
5	**leopard shark**	5½ ft (1¾ m)	Pacific coast of North America	no	least concern
5, 8	**wobbegong**	4 ft (1¼ m)	warm, shallow waters of the Indo-Pacific	unlikely	least concern
6–7, 9	**blue shark**	9 ft (2¾ m)	temperate and tropical waters worldwide	yes	near threatened
8	**dwarf lantern shark**	8 in (20 cm)	Caribbean Sea	no	data deficient
8, 27	*Stethacanthus*	2½ ft (76 cm)	worldwide (fossils)		extinct
8, 12, 29	**basking shark**	26 ft (8 m)	worldwide except for polar seas	no	endangered
8–9, 26–27, 29	*megalodon*	59 ft (18 m)	worldwide (fossils)		extinct
8	*Sarcoprion*	20 ft (6 m)	Greenland (fossils)		extinct
9, 13, 30	**tiger shark**	16 ft (5 m)	tropical and subtropical waters worldwide	yes	near threatened

*Explanation of conservation status terms (Source: IUCN Red List)

Extinct — no living individuals

Critically endangered — close to extinction

Endangered — high risk of extinction

Vulnerable — high risk of being endangered

Near threatened — likely to become endangered in the near future

Least concern — lowest risk; species is safe for now

Data deficient — not enough data to determine its risk of extinction

page number	name	average adult body length	range	dangerous to humans?	conservation status
9	**blacktip reef shark**	8 ft (2½ m)	tropical and subtropical waters of the Indo-Pacific	unlikely	near threatened
9	*Orthacanthus*	10 ft (3 m)	Europe and North America (fossils)		extinct
10	**sand tiger shark**	10 ft (3 m)	coastal waters worldwide	yes	vulnerable
10, 28, 29	**spiny dogfish shark**	40 in (1 m)	coastal waters worldwide	no	vulnerable
11	**swell shark**	35 in (90 cm)	coastal waters of the eastern Pacific Ocean	no	least concern
11	**Port Jackson shark**	5½ ft (1¾ m)	southern Australian ocean waters	unlikely	least concern
11	**greater spotted catshark**	5 ft (1½ m)	eastern Atlantic and Mediterranean Sea	no	near threatened
14	**bigeye thresher shark**	13 ft (4 m)	tropical waters worldwide	no	vulnerable
14, 31	**smoothback angel shark**	5 ft (1½ m)	Atlantic coast of Africa and Mediterranean Sea	no	critically endangered
15	**nurse shark**	10 ft (3 m)	tropical waters of the Atlantic and eastern Pacific	unlikely	vulnerable
15	**cookiecutter shark**	20 in (½ m)	tropical waters worldwide	unlikely	least concern
23	**longnose sawshark**	4½ ft (1½ m)	southern Australian ocean waters	no	least concern
24	**velvet belly lantern shark**	18 in (45 cm)	eastern Atlantic and Mediterranean Sea	no	least concern
26	*Helicoprion*	25 ft (7½ m)	worldwide (fossils)		extinct
28, 29	**Greenland shark**	21 ft (6½ m)	northern Atlantic Ocean and Arctic Ocean	no	near threatened
29	**Portuguese dogfish**	3 ft (1 m)	coastal waters of Atlantic and Indo-Pacific	no	near threatened
29	**pocket shark**	5½ in (14 cm)	deep Pacific waters off Chile	no	data deficient
31	**natal shyshark**	20 in (50 cm)	coastal waters of South Africa	no	vulnerable
31	**Ganges shark**	70 in (178 cm)	rivers of eastern India	no	critically endangered

Bibliography

The Encyclopedia of Sharks. By Steve Parker. Firefly Books, 2008.

Please Be Nice to Sharks: Fascinating Facts about the Ocean's Most Misunderstood Creatures. By Matt Weiss. Sterling Children's Books, 2016.

A Pocket Guide to Sharks of the World. By Dr. David A. Ebert and Dr. Sarah Fowler. Princeton University Press, 2015.

Shark. DK Eyewitness Books. By Miranda Macquitty. DK Children, 2008.

The Shark Handbook, Second Edition: The Essential Guide for Understanding the Sharks of the World. By Greg Skomal. Cider Mill Press, 2016.

Smart About Sharks! By Owen Davey. Flying Eye Books, 2016.

Super Shark Encyclopedia: And Other Creatures of the Deep. By Derek Harvey. DK Children, 2015.

The Ultimate Book of Sharks. By Brian Skerry. National Geographic Children's Books, 2018.